FINISHING LINE PRESS

www.finishinglinepress.com

MERGING STAR HYPOTHESES

poetry by

Mary K O'Melveny

Finishing Line Press
Georgetown, Kentucky

MERGING STAR HYPOTHESES

Publisher: Leah Maines

Editor: Christen Kincaid

Cover Art: Betsy Stewart *Biocriticals No. 1* www.betsystewart.com

Author Photo: Susan L. Waysdorf

Cover Design: Elizabeth Anastasia O'Melveny

Printed in the USA on acid-free paper.
Order online: www.finishinglinepress.com
           also available on amazon.com

Author inquiries and mail orders:
Finishing Line Press
P. O. Box 1626
Georgetown, Kentucky 40324
U. S. A.

Table of Contents

III. SKYWALKING

IV. PRESENCE IN THE ABSENCE

For Baylor, Cameron, Eddie, Esme, Hannah Rose, Mirabelle and Nathan

"The more clearly we can focus our attention on the wonders and realities of the universe about us, the less taste we shall have for destruction."
—*Rachel Carson*

I. MERGING STAR HYPOTHESES

> "Our feeblest contemplations of the Cosmos stir us—there is tingling in the spine, a catch in the voice, a faint sensation, as if a distant memory, of falling from a height."
>
> —*Carl Sagan*

MERGING STAR HYPOTHESES

*According to a recent National Public Radio report, astronomers expect
a collision in four years between two stars in the Cygnus Constellation
that will be visible to the naked eye for people on earth.*

Today, I read about two stars
which will meet head-on in firestorms
while pulverized bits and fragments
shower down like iridescent rain.

Normally, such red hot events
have long cooled to icy fragments
by the time some telescopic
lens lets us peer through galaxies

looking for ancient trouble spots,
fissions frozen like snow crystals.
We are entranced by the idea,
like sneaking into a 3-D

movie where cinemascopic
pile-ups, punchings and perishings
leave us breathless, lucky to be alive.
Of course, we are used to real time

conflagrations here: buildings topple,
deserts burn, crops vanish, cities
drown, lights dim, icebergs go missing.
Most days, we barely notice.

Eventually, echoes of our
losses thin out like errant fog.
As we stare skyward, awaiting
these star crashes, we discover

how future stargazers, thrilled
by gaudy sparks filling the skies
like holiday pyrotechnics,
might watch our own fierce flameout.

GHOST WHISPERERS

Scientists in observatories around the world, from Russia's
Caucasus Mountains to the South Pole, are trying to capture
the smallest subatomic particle of matter known as neutrinos.
They are believed to carry information from the beginnings
of the universe. "Observatory," New York Times, *July 12, 2018 D2.*

Neutrinos. They sound
like creatures that might
once have decorated some
great grandmother's woolen
coat collar. Instead, they
surround us, light as morning air,
sailing through universal matter
like microscopic fireflies.
They have disappeared within
atoms, protons, electrons,
filtered through like phantasma.
They have blazed trails
from the center of the sun
past dust from exploded stars.
They have *tap tap tap* danced
in and out of black holes,
cruised through planets
as if they were cirrus clouds.
Nothing stops them.
They have stories.
Big Bang broadsides.
Meteorological memoirs.
Earth's scientists gather
in caves, mines, ice mountains
hoping for a quantum whisper
that might clue us in on how
our reality took shape.
As we try to translate
their extraterrestrial tales,
we hope there is still time.

EVENING STAR

I saw you lingering
at horizon's dark edge.
Stepping up from sea foam,
casting long shadows.

Where were you when our need
was so great? Feminine
powers disappeared East.
Male sun rose to the West.

Everyone should have known
there were consequences
of staying home,
of staying *pure*.

Now your lightening
signature glows over
metal cages filled with
Mylar blanketed children.

Darkness has replaced lightning's glow.
Gloomy skies have shuttered
our vision. Dusk stands
down without an aureole's embrace.

FIRST NIGHT OF THE SUPERMOON
Del Ray Beach, Florida 11-13-16 (After the Election)

I stare up. It is unmistakable.
Superior. Sharp. Lustrous. It hovers
at ocean's edge. King tides sweep the waters
back and forth, as if cleansing the coarse sand.

As lightness vanished, we became bereft.
Perhaps this moon of grander proportions
is just what we need—an education in
alignments, orbits or phased rotations.

Old trajectories have lost their power
to comfort us. We stare in disbelief
as wilding waves surge, churn, hopes tossed
away like sea foam in chilled waters.

Darkness lurks behind this boldest lunar
incandescence. No woman has walked on
that icy surface. I crave reflections
of sunlight. Very near, yet still so far.

STAR WARS (FROM A TO Z)

In early June, 2016, scientists and archeologists reported findings that some of the spears and daggers uncovered in King Tut's tomb in 1925 had been constructed out of materials from crashed meteorites. X-ray fluorescence spectrometry was used to compare the iron in one of the daggers to 20 different meteorites known to have fallen during the time of Tut's reign in areas from the Sahara desert to Iran. An apparent match was found between the King's dagger and the nickel and cobalt contained in a meteorite nicknamed Kharga, which fell from the sky thousands of years ago near the port of Alexandria and was discovered in 2000. http://www.telegraph.co.uk/news/2016/06/01/tutankhamuns-blade-made-from-meteorite-study-reveals/. Earlier scientific analyses revealed that tools and weapons in areas of the world from Greenland to Russia were also built out of debris crashing to earth from outer space. http://www.hngn.com/articles/60572/20150115/meteorite-used-prehistoric-eskimos-before-introduction-iron.htm.

I.

Arcing at an improbable angle,
Bright white and burning,
Chasing stars
Down, dawns coming and going.
Eventually,
Far, far
Greater than anything known before,
Hotter and harder,
It,
Just (like the proverbial
Kryptonite),
Lands in a
Meadow.
No one who approaches it
Owns the original story. They may
Pray.
Question history.
Run.
Stop, stare.
Their hopes

Used up,
Visions settle in.
Wondering at mysteries,
aXes and daggers are constructed.
Young Warriors wave their arms, filled with
Zest for the wars they will wage.

II.

After the
Battles, a
Cleansing of souls
Descends.
Every lost but still living soldier
Finds
Gravitas
Holding high the
Interstellar
Javelin,
Knowing that the
Light of old stars has
Mixed, melted
Nimbly (perhaps numbly),
Over other soldiers whose
Pugilistic pageants matched their own,
Quests also not quite complete.
Ramming into Alexandrian earth, these
Stones spoke for long dark suns,
Terra firma enhanced by more
Universal energies. No more
Vainglorious ventures. Perhaps they were
Wiser up there where
eXtraterrestrial miracles became their own
Youthful
Zeitgeists.

III.

A king,
Born to fame,
Cradles his otherworldly
Dagger as he is prepared for
Eternal rest.
Friends, foes
Genuflect before
His
Images.
Jeweled
Knives are wrapped,
Laid down with care.
Men weep
Near Tut's tomb.
Others kneel
Piously,
Quiet,
Reverent.
Songs are sung.
Tributes trail along to the
Underground
Vaults
Where
X-rays will reveal,
Years and years later, still
Zealous echoes of royal armaments.

IF I WERE THE SUN

On August 12, 2018, NASA launched a $1.5 billion mission to "touch" the sun using the Parker Solar Probe. The spacecraft, traveling at 39,500 miles per hour, will first execute seven flybys of Venus, using that planet's gravitational force to catapult itself closer to the corona of the Sun. By 2024, scientists hope the satellite will come within 3.83 million miles—closer than any previous spacecraft. It will circle the Sun, at speeds approaching 430,000 miles per hour, measuring its corona during each orbit from many different locations. to determine how the Sun achieves temperatures as high as 27 million degrees Farenheit, as well as the origins of solar winds and flares which can affect the viability of life on Earth. The success of the mission depends on whether the probe's heat shield can protect temperature-sensitive delicate instruments on board. https://www.nasa.gov/content/goddard/parker-solar-probe

Whenever I have visitors, I ask all my little
stars to sit down, be hushed. Deny that my light
can dim. I insist upon respect for my radiance,
collective reverence for my omnipotence.

I know I am a star too but I am so much bigger
than everyone else. And far more important,
in the scheme of things. I become furious
when other suns disagree, when they

see me as just one more little star
surrounded by old and long forgotten
pinheads of white. Really Sad!
My storms and heat are the extremest EVER.

I am the greatest pretender.
I can preen and shine past the best of them.
I know it is my visage that sets the world alight,
at least in this little world,

where no one else is here to contradict me.
I look pretty important up here. Resplendent, in fact.
I hiss and fizz and spit out fiery commands.

No one gets near me without third degree damage.

Those who have tried are vaporized
before they can turn around or change their mind.
They were pillars of salt, melting into my orbit.
There is no sorry up here. No do-overs.

Today, I am the sky king and homage is required.
I must insist upon it. OR ELSE!!
If you thought I might vanish, word could spread
that I am not permanent,

not omnipotent, not much more
than some ancient conflagration.
You must cover your eyes as darkness falls.
My need for revenge ignites me.

By the time you arrive at my doorstep,
I will blow right past your ashes
on my way to greater, more luminous places.
All fueled by white heat.

But you appear to think otherwise.
You claim you will discover the real me,
learn how to douse my fires until they flatten out
like lumps of camp stove ashes.

I say you can investigate me all you want
but you cannot starve me of the atmosphere
that fuels me. I am in charge and you are nothing
new. How did you get up here anyway?

WHEN BLACK HOLES COLLIDE

*Sounds created by colliding black holes millions of years ago are now
being heard around the world by astronomers and astrophysicists
using data from Laser Gravitational Wave Observatories (LIGO). This
data confirms many of Einstein's 20th century findings, including the
Theory of Relativity.*

Scientists are listening
To the sound track
Of the Universe.

Einstein proves right again.
Ripples of gravity travel
Through dust, wind, darkness,

Stirring up space-time
Like a celestial stew
Where everything is in the mix

But no one knows
What will emerge
When expansion ends.

We can see past light.
Chirps of sound bend,
Twist, turn, tumble,

Lead us backward
To celestial rumbles
In dark corners

Of long dead skies.
Colliding neutron stars
Transform past and present.

As gravitational death
Concerts entertain us,
Each shriek, scream, shout

Tells a tale of tumult.
What fanfare will
follow earth's departure?

ANOTHER TAKE ON ANTI-MATTER

Anti-matter cannot coexist with matter so it is difficult to study.
NASA has examined the Milky Way and other distant galaxies to try
to detect it. A recent laser experiment allowed scientists to briefly
measure it. Antimatter is considered to be a trigger mechanism for
nuclear weapons. http://www.independent.co.uk/news/science.

I've been ruminating
about the properties
of dark anti-matter.
Or, put another way,
White House election results.

What if Big Bang theories
were wrong? What if anti-
particles just arrived now,
rather than when the world
began?

As we slowly
evolved, we learned
how to bind, to combine
energies in our observable worlds.
All things seemed quite possible.

Now, instability
hovers everywhere,
particle collisions
a daily occurrence.
Gamma ray signatures

are colliding here while
NASA scientists search
far off galaxies for stellar remnants.
Why don't they look at black holes
in near space instead?

IN LESS THAN THE TIME TO
SPEAK OUT THEIR NAMES

—After Orlando

Astronomers have opened up windows
to the universe. We can hear black holes
colliding. A cataclysmic cosmos.
Gravitational waves chirping energy
from dark events circling and spinning out.

Pulses from long devoured universes.
Faint noises of vast doom-filled moments,
where annihilation also happened quickly,
spell out destruction light years later.
Vibrations of loss surround us.

KILONOVAS

A Kilonova is a transient astronomical event occurring when two neutron stars or a neutron star and a black hole merge into each other. In 2017, astronomers heard the sounds of kilonovas colliding 130 million light years away.

Today we hear the clatter of worlds colliding.
Half of us were holding our breaths,
as our bodies coiled backwards in fear,
shame settled on our skin like cheap perfume.

Half of us were holding our breaths
while the rest of us were shrieking.
Shame settled on our skin like cheap perfume
as we waited for someone to hear us.

While the rest of us were shrieking,
someone was always shaking with outrage.
As we waited for someone to hear us,
we were told to be silent, move on, laugh it off.

Someone was always shaking with outrage
even when we were bruised and battered.
We were told to be silent, move on, laugh it off.
Did we ask for it? Did we make it up?

Even when we were bruised and battered,
we were muzzled by messages of objectivity.
Did we ask for it? Did we make it up?
Or did the noise of humiliation deafen everyone?

We were muzzled by messages of objectivity.
No one wanted to know the sounds of grief.
Or did the noise of humiliation deafen everyone?
Our tormentors basked in celestial rhythms.

No one wanted to know the sounds of grief.
But now we see their days were numbered.

Our tormentors basked in celestial rhythms.
Today we hear the clatter of worlds colliding.

ICARUS

NASA's Hubble Space Telescope recently detected a giant blue superstar which casts light that has taken 9 billion years to reach the planet Earth. The star, named "Icarus," looks to observers the way it would have appeared when the universe was only about one third of its current age. It is believed to be twice as hot as our Sun. http://www. astronomy.com/news/2018/04/hubble-images-farthest-star-ever-seen.

Above us, a blue star's aura
has entered our point of view.
Its nine billion year pathway
likely more fixed than the journey
of its namesake—unknown, unsung
as flight began. We are far from
first to follow its florescence
or feel its incinerating flame.

One imagines early tales told
as the star first passed: gods displeased,
fairies appeased, sounds of lament
or exultation sung by priests
and elders, to be later re-told
by more cavalier travelers sincere
in their belief that they knew
everything there was to know.

Perhaps some observers were humbled
by each new sighting, while others
looked elsewhere, soared higher
for cheap thrills, then dropped
helplessly into the sea as loved ones
watched in horror. At each point
in this stellar poetic debut, someone
decided whether to seek incandescence
or opt for a safe, steady glide.

SUNSTONES

Danish archeologists believe that the Vikings used Calcite crystals to see patterns of polarized light so they could locate the sun. This enabled them to navigate in overcast and dark weather and travel to uncharted territories long before the invention of the magnetic compass. (See nytimes.com/04-10-18/ "Norse GPS").

Sometimes I feel we have become Vikings,
traveling the world without a compass,
our ships foundering on foggy oceans.

Yet, some say those Norsemen used magical
stones to help them navigate darkening
waters, reading play of light across vast skies,

turning them over in calloused hands as
canopies of gloom hovered above sails,
each beam spitting out phosphorescent sparks.

Today's journeys to new worlds are different,
freedom's glow now thin as smoke at dusk.
Instead of searching for sunshine, refugees

hunker down at world's edge like
Cimmerians embracing dark places.
One imagines Eric the Red landing

in Greenland after seeking patterns
in crystals, his arrival lauded by
optimists open to change and challenge.

Today, as we turn away travelers
shadowed by fears in darkened skies,
the luster of polarized light has vanished.

AURORA BOREALIS

The sun's many magnetic fields distort and twist as it rotates on its axis. Sometimes these fields become knotted together, then burst creating sunspots. Often, such sunspots occur in pairs; the largest can be several times the size of earth's diameter. Boils and bubbles are created when the sun's temperature rises and falls (which can be 27 million degrees Fahrenheit). During that process, particles escape from surface sunspots, hurling plasma particles known as solar wind into space. These winds can reach the earth in about 40 hours and, when they do, they cause the dramatic light displays known as the aurora borealis, also known as "the Northern Lights." When sunspot particles collide with oxygen, vivid colors of yellow and green are produced, while interactions with nitrogen produce striking pink, red, violet, and occasionally blue colors. The most dramatic displays occur approximately every eleven years. Scientists believe these displays are also visible from other planets in our solar system. http://www.space.com

Some say you should never
wave, whistle or sing while
viewing the Northern Lights.
Specters will find you. Troubles
follow. Others endorse
claps or shouts so you can
commune with the ancestors,
enjoy their stellar songs.

I'd prefer silence as
dawn's goddesses stir up
their fragrant stew spiced
with sage, basil, cinnamon
or sing to north winds in
tones of topaz, ruby
that echo like jeweled stones
skimming across water.

Perhaps these lights really are
spirits dancing—souls in search
of respite, fire foxes creating

sparks as their tales brush snow
from mountains, the armor glow
of Valkyries leading warriors
toward Valhalla. Everyone
has a guess. No one knows.

But I do know it is not enough
to simply stare at skies turned
to gardens of orchid,
periwinkle, carnation,
mulberry, fuchsia. What if
this rainbowed architecture holds
creation's keys? How might we
embrace its incendiary tales?

SUPER BLOOD WOLF MOON ECLIPSE

Once again, Mother Nature dazzled
with her supernatural prowess.
Our night skies lit us all up
like too many blood orange cocktails,

then dimmed down like eyes lowered
in prayerful thoughts that too much
drink can conjure. As earth slid
between moon and sun, cuddled in

like a hopeful barroom patron
looking for a late night hook up,
a slow blush began to brush our cheeks,
then fanned out to an old drunk's rosacea.

This fiery moment lasted longer
than some hurried embrace offered
with a morning's regret. I say we
celebrate our luck among stars,

stare beyond our seamy planet
into that deep place where wolves howl,
before hope, like July fireflies,
scatters in a flash of rubies.

PLEASE CHIME IN

A powerful new telescope, the Canadian Hydrogen Intensity Mapping Experiment (CHIME), recently picked up repeating bursts of sound believed to emanate from distant galaxies located 1.5 to 3 billion light years away. Scientists believe these "fast radio bursts" (FRBs) are "pops" of low-frequency radiation generated by powerful magnetic fields. New York Times, *January 11, 2019, A18.*

These days, pops of sound are scary,
especially when we want quiet.
But I am intrigued by some news
from far away percussive space:

Our cosmos is layered with noise.
Fast radio bursts *buzz, sizzle.*
Astronomers hear aerial
razzle dazzle from some distant

galaxy's caterwauling mass
of gas. As black holes bluster, blast,
we strain for meaning here on earth.
Drumming sounds of constant deceit

leave us dumbed down, discordant notes
all around. With truth's rhythms in
retreat, universal broadcasts
of new songs delight. Let us dance.

II. THEORIES OF RELATIVITY

"There are as many atoms in a single molecule of your DNA as there are stars in the typical galaxy. We are, each of us, a little universe."

—*Neil deGrasse Tyson*

"Each one of you can change the world, for you are made of star stuff, and you are connected to the universe."

—*Vera Rubin*

ON THE DAY OF THE SOLAR ECLIPSE

I.
My wife and I did not stare up at the sun
as it turned to darkness. We should have
looked for eclipse glasses well beforehand.
Call us lazy. Or optimists
who believed stores would not run out.
Instead, we looked out our kitchen window
at the grassy dappled yard below.
Waited for everything to change.

Luckily, NASA chronicled the
journey so we could briefly turn
into scientists as we strived to
understand our tentative places
in vast skies. We crossed the continent—
Oregon, Illinois, the Carolinas—
to stay with crowds in dark glasses
cheering a rare sight of national unity.

Back in our actual range of
vision, the light turned silvery
like it might on a foggy day.
Otherwise, we saw little change.
Traffic passed, trash was tossed, phones
were checked, conversations resumed.
Still, imagination's limits had briefly
shifted toward something new and full.

II.
My third grade Science Fair project—
a cardboard box rigged up with balls and lights.
The moon's slow trajectory toward the sun.
Light to dark. Crescents contracted and expanded.

My father had helped me build it. Scientific
expertise had trumped an eight year old's search
for her own conclusions. It won a prize.

But I felt as fraudulent as a shadow.

Now, my memories of him are so slimmed down,
so untrustworthy, that I cannot recall the moment
when the prize was bestowed. I do not know
if he was proud or just resigned to my inadequacies.

We packed up the box and put it in our car.
My blue ribbon grew tattered over the years, finally
disappeared, leaving behind a corona of wishful thinking
that we might have tried harder to see each other.

III.
My scientist brother tells me how he stood
in his yard, binoculars rigged up for his
near total view. He lives so high in Colorado's
hills that mountain lions walk on his porch.

Our distances have increased over time.
Our genetic connections seem as shadowy
as dimming candles. Still, some connections
emerge. Last night, a bear walked on my driveway.

Briefly aligned by solar trajectories,
promises of incandescence soon faded.
We drifted away once more
Like vaporous gasses of the sun.

THE MATHEMATICS OF PARKING

My parking skills are excellent.
People comment often
on my ability to slide in
to the smallest spaces.
A quick wheel turn or two,
it's done. I walk away.

My father taught me to park.
A lesson in pure geometry.
Mathematics determined
most of his daily moves.
Like making all the beds
with only hospital corners.

The beauty of calculus,
or so he would say,
was in having the right answers.
Careful proofs produced satisfaction.
Anything else fell short,
left everyone disappointed.

Perhaps his great anger
grew from our quite human limitations.
Pen to paper, word to ear
not always a numeric certainty.
Instead, we struggled to relate.
Formulas elusive, answers clouded.

Home from World War II,
he had already lost interest
in succession. He wanted out,
hoped to move on. Instead,
he got three kids. Six heart attacks.
Algorithmic bad luck.

We never liked each other much.
My mother cried too often.

I tried to compute the statistical relationship
between his presence or absence
and the sadness that filled our rooms.
It was significant.

I remember driving with my
mother over dark mountain roads
to the VA Hospital ER.
Siblings boarded with neighbors.
I could never tell if the substance
filling the car was fear or relief.

Somehow he beat death again.
Like a savvy gambler
shaving with a plastic razor
in the casino bathroom,
smiling into the mirror, red–rimmed
eyes smarting from morning light.

Later on, the numbers did run out.
Someone retrieved me from
my college English class
to deliver the somber news.
I am older now than he was then,
with lists of questions

I never asked. And answers
I think might be correct.
But who can ever know?
Our universes did not compute.
What might we say
to each other now,

taking careful measure,
like long-dead stars
realigning briefly
to see if logic mattered.

I know one thing I would say:
Thanks for the parking lessons.

SPATIAL RELATIONS

Some days one can look around
at siblings and families
and wonder—*who are these people?*

Hasn't every kid thought
about *adoption?* Waited to be told
about a hospital switch?

Or, perhaps the other way around:
looked furtively for other options—leaving
with strangers at a rest stop or a library?

Maybe this happens more
when families are too small,
every frailty on full display,

no way to get lost in crowds
of siblings or cousins where din
of shouts or laughter obscures angst.

I had always imagined the joys
of family reunions—parents smiling,
jolly aunts and uncles setting out

food-filled picnic tables centered by
red and white checkered cloths,
everyone telling new versions of their pasts.

Instead, the few cousins I ever knew of
lived across the continent, rarely visited,
eventually disappeared altogether.

Once I found a box filled with misty photos,
a hodgepodge of blurred history. Some images
radiated. Others were as inscrutable as silent strangers.

I saw vague hints in a handful—a glint of eye,

my mother's brow, my father's frown,
a profile with an upswept hairdo that forecast

my grandmother's later independent
take on the world. My great grandfather,
sitting behind his railroad office desk,

eyes obscured by an eyeshade, a slight smile
forming. Perhaps it was taken just before
a scorned husband shot him dead there.

These celluloid chronicles rested in my closet
for years. Now and then, I tried to decipher
faded handwriting, as if we could still be introduced.

Eventually I gave up, mailed these photos
of vanishing bloodlines to my brother.
He plans to meet everyone whenever he gets to Heaven.

He expects it to be crowded up there,
everyone dressed up in photo-shoot finery.
I figured this would give him a head start.

THEORIES OF RELATIVITY

I have been thinking about families.
Whether blood, bone, ligament form deepest
connections just because some genetic
matter floated by at speed of light.

When I was growing up, it seemed our family
was all adrift, heavy elements exploding.
Some days, we moved tentatively, evaluating our
relationships to everyone else. On others, free fall.

Outside his foxhole, my father railed at us.
Camel cigarette smoke filled
the air like spectral visions.
He was a lesson in electromagnetic force.

My mother cowered in corners,
pretending to be calm even as new flames
sparked up around us. Maybe she hoped
firefighters would save us all from ourselves.

As a kid at our dinner table, I tried
to decipher which words were forces
of attraction and reaction. Often, as time slowed,
I felt closest to the family dog.

Greying now, I am still pondering
such queries. As earth rotates beneath
my feet, equal claims to Supernova
powers lie with my families of choice.

My wife, whose steady hand has guided
our travels like a time machine conductor.
My friends, who know that compassion's
quantity must always exceed light speed.

The apple may not fall far from the tree
but the orchards are wide as galaxies.

I want connective energies to equal
a central mass of tenderness.

Our loss of any loved one feels
more profound than speeding rays,
genomes or not. We don't want goodbyes.
We want to bend their light.

FISSION (Or, The Day I Discovered My Wife—June, 1988)

> *Radioactive fission, where the center of a heavy element spontaneously emits a charged particle as it breaks down into a smaller nucleus, does not occur often, and happens only with the heavier elements. Fission is different from the process of fusion, when two nuclei join together rather than split apart.* —Live Science.

Was it fission or fusion?
Either way, I felt its
spontaneity. Charged particles
blew into the vestibule where
we had been standing. The hairs
on my arms rose up as if
an electrical storm was
brewing right over grey
carpeted halls and pastel
prints decorating white walls.

We had been working late
on legal documents, studying
citations as if they were Talmudic
texts, trying to hone the nucleus
of our arguments. Suddenly,
all air vanished from the room.
Sound would not carry. Looking
back, I am not sure what words could
have traversed those light years

that had traveled between us
in that moment of raw energy.
Suddenly, reactions fed fires,
let loose, tumbled out, then
re-emerged larger than before.
All I remember now is that
life as I had known it was over.
My new self was about to expand,
proliferate like a nuclear firestorm.

ICE SKATING ON THE MOON (On the Day After...)

I dreamt we went
ice skating   on
the darkest side
of the moon   where
no one could find
us   where water-
filled comets fell
and no one heard
a sound   we were
hidden so deep
in penumbras
deep space probes
missed our sparkle
the magic arc
of our brazen
triple axels

dark poles hid us
solar windstorms
dropped frost crystals
we leapt to catch
them   before they
could show up on
radio waves   we were
determined to
stay submerged
to swirl   to leap
to places where
no could find us
where we would be
audacious
free of judgments
pure as crystals

THE UMBRA AROUND US

These days, the eclipse is on
our minds. I don't mean the one
involving the sun.
I'm worried about kindness
dimming, eroding faster
than sand dunes or coral reefs.

The other day, my wife and I
were driving home, a rainbow
sticker peeking out from our bumper,
when two young white men
began shrieking invectives, fingers.
piercing air like pitchforks.

Rage shrouded their eyes.
Tattoos covered their arms,
skulls and swastikas swarmed.
Maybe they were heading down
to Charlottesville. Maybe diminishment
has always defined them.

Now, they have swollen up,
intent on blotting out everything
that is not them. Suddenly, shadows
hover everywhere. Penumbras
and umbras arrive unannounced
as we are sitting peaceably

on our front stoops
or holding signs of protest.
Even as our world darkens,
we still stare heavenward.
We keep trying to ignore shadows,
to hope blindness will not follow.

SLIPPING BELOW THE SURFACE

My brother-in-law drowned looking for bluefish.
His mother said drowning was a death preferred
by Kings. Looking around her living room,
weeping submerging us all, royalty felt distant.

We all wanted to be transported skyward, shouting
questions to the gods about decisions beyond our ken.
Aegaeon, god of violent storms, seemed suited
to our quest yet he lay quiet as our tears kept on.

Ceto and Cymopoleia, goddesses of waves
and torrents, could well have spoken up
but they too stayed still, unable to explain our loss
or give comfort to the keening widow.

As for watery graves, perhaps there are more
regal moments than we were privy to that sad
summer afternoon. But one doubts it can be so.
Sadness reigns even in celestial palaces.

My friend of many years died in a rip tide,
forever altering my view of ocean vistas,
white sand beachfronts and vacation getaways.
Once again, meaning eluded survivors

huddled together on dry land. No royals
showed up to ponder the peacefulness
of the demise as the bereft gasped for air,
flailed their arms, helpless against fate's currents.

Each day now, from temporary survival's
relative safety, our newspapers spill out
statistics of failed optimism, escapes
from sorrows greater than we have known—

children fight for breath as sarin gases
fill their lungs, homes sink into rubble,

families swallowed by whirlpools of war,
vanish in smoke at markets and schoolyards.

Escapees drown in multiples of multiples.
Yellow life rafts capsize on turquoise seas,
tattered orange life vests and scraps of colored flags
fan out like crown jewels over frigid waters.

GOLDILOCKS AND...

In May, 2016, new data from NASA's Kepler space telescope revealed the existence of 1,284 new planets orbiting Sun-like stars in the Milky Way, the closest of which could be 12 light years away from Earth. Based on information about those planets, Astronomists and Astrobiologists have determined that at least nine may orbit in their Sun's habitable zone where, given sufficient atmospheric pressure, the planetary surface and average temperatures can support liquid water for a period long enough to generate life. This zone is also known as the "Goldilocks Zone" because the region around the star must not be too hot or too cold but rather "just right," as was the porridge in the children's fable "Goldilocks and the Three Bears." NASA launched its Kepler telescope in 2009 and it has been regularly discovering new planets ever since. See, e.g., www.cnn.com /2016/05/10/health/nasa-kepler-discoveries.

My deck is littered with glass,
twisted metal, tortured hooks.
A flurry of outrage
greets me—Cardinals,
Finches, Jays and Doves—
Where is breakfast?

I had begun to pull back
from their wintry feasts. A longer
sun casts light on other prey.
Yet I like to watch them as they politely
wait their turns, a few modest thoughts
sparking out from eager beaks.

The crime scene deck is twenty feet
off the ground. We did not dream
the calculations of that climb.
My trellises lie crumpled like paper,
claw mark hieroglyphics rise up and up,
speaking volumes of triumph and conquest.

The Mother and her two cubs must be large.
Roaming the yard earlier, they picked off
all lower hanging birdseed banquets,

rolled around with their spoils
in the thick of night,
glistened in shine of moonlight.

The newest planetary discoveries
sizzle and shimmer in some time frame
lost to us. Scientists peer into
super telescopes, hoping to find signs
of life as we might know it Eons later
in the Goldilocks zone of Sun-like stars.

I want to know if my three adventurous
marauders might just as easily
laugh out there in that not too hot,
not too cold night, lit by some distant Moon,
as they execute their stealthy tour de force,
all around them sleeping.

RAGE (Or, Watching Senate Hearings)

I am filled up with it.
I could float to the Moon.
And beyond. To places
no one has ever gone.

How can one stop anger
that is sparked back up by
each new day's outrages,
every pore blazing?

First, I snapped off the tv,
cancelled the newspapers,
switched the radio dial
to Mozart and Fauré.

When that did not work,
I raced to the ocean, hoping
it could douse my ire
as my grey hair turned scarlet.

Next, I sat down in my woods
but had to leave, fearing
forest conflagrations
too large to be put down

by mortal firefighters
used to dealing with a
forgotten cigarette
or a careless camper.

I walked out to my garden,
ripped out some weeds, threw
down some seeds, watched for hope
as flirting birds flew past.

Not even summer rain
could bring down my body

temperature. Everything I knew
flashed red hot like a raw wound.

Turns out, looking skyward
is best. I must search for Vulcan,
ask him how thunderbolts
can be forged from my flesh.

LASER VISIONS

On Tuesday, October 2, 2018, the Nobel Prize in Physics was awarded to three scientists for their work harnessing pure light into a force that could manipulate microscopic objects and investigate properties of atoms and other elusive entities. During the same week, the FBI pursued an "investigation" into allegations of sexual assault made by Dr. Christine Blasey Ford against the President's nominee for the Supreme Court.

They give Nobel prizes
to those who transform light
to chirps, drills and pulses.
Light that manipulates
microscopic objects,
punches past dense surfaces.

These optical toolkits
can ferret out atoms
and viruses, or solve
mysteries of disease
like some luminous sleuth
whose monochromatic

light waves reveal inner
villains. Such science might
alter our destinies.
Imagine it: a beam
shines on two people.
Her truths light up the room.

FINGERPRINTS

Microorganism
pigments provide life clues
on orbiting star surfaces

as light spirals, spins, stamps
each cosmic chronicle.

DaVinci's inky brown
thumbprint was recently
found at Windsor Castle.

A parchment sketch, a woman's
body, near her left arm.

Imagine the moment—
cadaver splayed beneath
him. As he shifts paper,
grasps it with his thumb,

perhaps he peers closer,
to see if her face might
warrant a sketch as well.

Last night I placed my
thumb against your left arm.

What trace of that act was left
behind? I want to believe
that you would remember
my touch as if inked there.

We have no masterpiece status.
This stroke only matters now.

REMEMBERING "TREES"

Joyce Kilmer's poem "Trees" was first published in 1914. Kilmer died at the age of 32 in World War I. He wrote three books of poetry.

a poem as lovely as
a mouth as hungry as
a breast as sweet as
a prayer as
a robin's nest as
a bosom as
a life as
a god as

joyce kilmer was
the first poet I ever
knew about
a rare bonding event
with my father
as we stood
in a pine forest
on a cold fall day

as I shivered
watched starlings soar
and colored leaves
roll around like fiesta confetti
my stern father began
to recite each word
soft sweet
like a flower seller

he had me repeat
each line until I knew
more than
I had ever known
about trees
or god
or the breathless magic
of poetry

III. SKYWALKING

"Somewhere, something incredible is waiting to be known."

—Carl Sagan

SKYWALKING

In March, 2013, a young mother of a ten month old baby jumped from
the window of her 8-story Manhattan apartment. She had strapped her
son into a harness before leaping out. Her body cushioned the baby's fall
and he suffered only minor injuries. The mother, a lawyer, left behind 13
pages of handwritten notes scrawled on a yellow legal pad which were
found by her husband when he returned home.

What can be said
of opening a window,
bundling up her baby—
carefully strapping him to her—
clicking the ties into place?
Did she speak to him softly
before leaping into space?

Thirteen pages of notes,
filling up the yellow legal pad—
"I'm sorry"
"I am evil"
"I was afraid"
"Please forgive me for being so sad"
"My tears could not stop."

It was a sunny day,
a hint of breeze
curtains billowing
in a small, hardly noticeable way.
Neighbors took their laundry down,
a doorman let in a delivery man,
elevators traversed their universe.

How did her journey begin? Was her mind
already lost before she pulled back the curtains?
Perhaps it was all so swift,
there were no moments for regret,
for second-guessing her spaceflight,
understanding that its weightlessness
would be temporary.

Imagine the journey down—

did she mourn two lives passing
before her eyes?
Pedestrians stop in distress,
disbelieving what descends.
The rushing air sounds like a train,
alarm bells long past hearing.

The street is unforgiving to her.
Such time travel rarely ends well.
Still, a miracle occurs—the baby boy
flies free of carnage, cushioned by his soft carrier
and his mother's flesh, he emerges
with a just bruise or two from his
brush with the speeding cosmos.

Later, the bewildered father
sits quietly, staring out the window
that will haunt him daily
until they move away.
He has read the yellow lined pages
over and over again, the words
from an alphabet he does not know.

As he cradles his son in his arms,
thankful for his second gift of life,
this strangest of synergies,
he wonders what will wake his son
years later from deep sleep.
Will he seek velocity or shy away
from the unknown?

Will he stare out airplane windows,
circadian rhythms wildly askew,
looking for reasons?
Looking for her?

JUNGLE KING ACOUSTICS

On May 2, 2016, 33 Lions landed at Oliver Tambo Airport in Johannesburg, South Africa. They were rescued from South American zoos where they had been raised and displayed in captivity for most of their lives and subjected to abuse and cruelty. They were rescued by the Animal Defenders Sanctuary, an international animal rights rescue organization. The Lions will live out the balance of their lives uncaged.

What does the sound of thirty-three Lions
landing at Oliver Tambo Airport
do to the rhythm of the universe?
Does it throw it off a millisecond
or so? A vibrant vibrato shaping
our future timing? Perhaps
it radiates out like sounds of Saturn
reaching out past its Rings.

I imagine a reverberation.
Roars pulse in our ears. Drumbeats
celebrate sudden space
where all was once small cages.
(I was once deafened by four Lions
on a Zambian preserve, air rich
with aftermath of a Rumble.
Licking their wounds, tails bristling.
Fight over. The lioness gone.)

The metal crates are hoisted down.
Dubious workers in overalls
peer in, eyes bright, stance guarded.
What must they think of each other?
Lions, used to limitations
and disappointments, waking up
from drugs and fear, have a thing or two
to say. Handlers just want all to go smoothly.

Soon, the lions arrive at Savannah grasses,
a wildness new to them.
Stepping out of their containers,

they hear their own music, round and full,
anger on the borders for those who broke their teeth,
took their claws. Bellowing now, they call,
cry, howl, holler, thunder, wail
way, way out past the Moon.

PIANO MAN

Paul Barton, a self-taught British pianist and painter, moved to Thailand in 1966 to teach piano. He became involved with Elephants World, a wildlife sanctuary on the banks of the River Kwai in Kanchanabury, which is home to elephants formerly used and abused in Thailand's logging industry and as tourist attractions. Many of the elephants are blind, disabled and psychologically damaged. Paul regularly plays piano for these rescued elephants on a nearby mountainside. His story is told in an award-winning documentary, "Music for Elephants."

A blind bull elephant,
his mouth full of barna
grass, picks up his head, turns
toward the sounds of Bach
scaling mountain breezes
like a snowy egret.

Another, tusks broken,
toenails slashed like tires in
a junkyard, stops mid-climb
to lift his heavy trunk.
He sways with a chorale
like a seasoned conductor.

More gather by the man
at the wooden upright
he has planted in the
bush as gently as if
it were a parlor salon
where draperies rustle

and crystal goblets clink.
Soon Mozart joins them all
in an arc of pink gold
sunset and softening air.
Nothing holds them here but
a pianist's nimble hands.

Before forest havens
vanished, they ruled with
resonance. Perhaps these
notes call back tales once told
in jungle darkness, as stars
riffed, trilled, danced above them.

A GUIDE TO ECHOLOCATION

For Louis M. Herman, a scientist whose seminal research revealed that dolphins could understand and respond to human language transmitted by sound and visual signals.

I.
A man who had tried talking to dolphins
from his science lab in Yokahama Bay
died the other day, not
because he tried to talk
or because they tried to listen,
but only because death happens.

Dolphins, it turns out,
have many things to say about death.
They have been riding with death
ever since the days of Minoan seafarers
whose clumsy drawings of their exploits
filled up walled murals with magical thinking.

II.
Aphrodite traveled on their backs.
Dionysus turned them from pirate
thieves to rescuers of sailors.
Arion of Lesbos sang to them
of his impending death
and they guided him home instead.

Apollo's thanks moved them to far skies
where the lingo of salvation always hovers.
There, they swim eastward of the Milky Way,
exchange street talk at the celestial equator,
dive, skim and rise again, flying over
Constellations of Heavenly Waters.

III.
It is said that Delphic oracles spoke
their oceanic predictions, recounted

amphibious tales of sweet redemption,
charted their intricate passages
to the fluid afterlife. Their sonnets
are recorded on Petra's red rock walls.

Poseidon called to them as well after dolphin
poems of love brought him his bride. He too
wrote his thank yous high above the seas.
Aelian and Homer tell tales of compassion and rescue.
No wonder humans lust for common language—
Rosetta Stones to open secrets of the sea.

IV.
Bottlenose pods must stare quizzically
from below their watery surfaces
at odd human antics—how they
so intently repeat the simplest tasks:
Fetch the ball. Touch the ring.
Carry the seaweed. Find the bomb.

Perhaps the dead scientist came to terms
with imagination's limits when
whistles, clicks and wheezes failed to flower
on dry land. But others still seek sonic
sonatas hiding beneath ocean waves,
as yet unknown in human lexicons.

V.
Half a century ago, a human woman loved
a dolphin. Forsaking all others, she made
him a watery home. His fins pressed her limbs,
he nosed past her breasts.
She felt his sounds of pleasure, sang back
to him in sweet signals of devotion and desire.

As with most experiments, love failed
to conquer all. Melodies and harmonies ceased.

Dolphins, it turns out, can also die of broken hearts.
Perhaps, as he sank down, down, down
beneath the silenced waters, never to speak again,
he understood abstraction *and* reality.

PERSEID METEOR SHOWERS

Sitting on the porch deck
in obscure night darkness,
I am searching the sky
for signs of shooting stars,

while thinking of deep sea
burials. Perseus,
grandson of Zeus,
adrift, floating to Seriphos.

Mother and son released,
dark oracle prophesies
submerged, the hero god's
trajectories begin.

Gorgon, sea monsters slain.
Pegasus born of their blood.
Andromeda rescued.
Athena victorious.

Yet, despite all, rescue
proves inadequate. He
cannot be saved from fate.
His great star flares, then falls.

TRAVELS TO THE VALLEY OF LOST THINGS

*Orlando Furioso was the hero of an epic poem written by Ludovio
Ariosto in 1516 using an ottava rima rhyme scheme. In the poem,
Orlando, one of Charlemagne's knights, goes mad when the woman he
loves betrays him. Another knight, Astolpho, flies to the moon—where
it is said all missing things can be found—in search of Orlando's wits.
In the original poem, Orlando's wits are recovered. Five hundred years
later, no cure has been found for dementia.*

It is said all missing things
might end up on the moon—
the royal battle gear of kings,
lesser leavings too—cups and spoons,
missing teeth or spectacles, slings
and arrows of heartbreak strewn
about like poetry fragments, ill-fated
once they left a lover unpersuaded.

My best friend's mind flew to pieces
like Orlando Furioso's. Flying
in a fiery chariot to that orbed precipice,
I became Astolfo. I sought clarifying
memories I hoped might well free us
both if we retrieved their edifying
truths. I feared they would be hidden
on the moon's dark side—forbidden

fruit for searchers who would rather
snatch up bits of sound, pretend they mean
something more than random blather.
If thoughts were stones, it seems
heft alone might assist a gatherer
bent on carrying home some gleam
of truth. Like a necklace breaking,
her cognition scattered to ground. Raking

thoughts back up like so many grains
of sand proved too difficult, despite
my zeal. It seems what is lost remains

so. Even my struggles with hindsight,
scattered throughout these lunar domains,
yielded little. I wanted to ignite
those flames of recollection needed
to return to lucid orbits that preceded
her collapsing persona. My intended

quest is doomed even on this landscape
rich with absent details. Nothing my friend did
or said can be unearthed in any shape
or form here. At last, I apprehended
how hope fades out. While I groped and gaped
at cerebral debris, even moonlight
had disappeared from her line of sight.

PORTRAIT OF A GAZAN STARGAZER

*An April 30, 2018 story by New York Times reporters Iyad Abuheweila
and David M. Halbfinger, recounts an interview with 22 year-old Gaza
City resident Saber al-Gerim whose days are spent lobbing rocks at Israeli
soldiers over the prison-like border fence. It doesn't matter if they shoot me
or not, Mr. al-Gerim said. Death or life—it's the same thing.*

I am the proud son of a beggar.
I have never seen our ancestral
lands. I can re-load my slingshot
with stones faster than olives drop
from the trees of my grandfather.
I have a scarf to cover up my
face when my eyes begin to sting
from tear gas or when burning
tire smoke catches in my throat.
I wrestle each day with barbed wire
as if it were a sordid thought
that could be swept from my mind's eye.
I have no job other than to
demand an end to the Nakba—
our forcible exile to lands
of no return. I have little
use for prayer and cannot bear
the cost of love. Our kitchen floor
is made of sand. I can build a fire
to cook eggplants and tomatoes.
I used to raise birds on our roof—
chickens and pigeons—but my winged
companions were soon felled by bombs.
To replace them, I learned to make
kites from plastic bags and paper
strips that can sail across fences
and berms to carry our messages.
I like to sleep in the desert
where star patterns suggest an open world.
I try to imagine how I would
traverse its pathways, my arms wide,
my voice filled with songs of longing.

INDEPENDENCE DAY

If I were a Native American,
what would I be doing today?
While flags were waving toward
a bluest sky filled with whitest clouds.
While charcoal grills were firing up,
smoke pouring out into crisp afternoon air.

Maybe I get the day off because it was
the anniversary of a time when white men
proclaimed to other white men how tired they were
of being disrespected. They laid down some rules
about the boundaries that cannot be crossed
as my people watched our lands slip away.

Maybe I place some wood on my own fire,
pull a beer from the fridge and look out
over the ridge of trees that shelter my ancestors.
Listen to some blues on my old radio.
Maybe I tap my feet to lonesome tales
of two timing and strings of broken hearts.

Or perhaps I begin to plan again for resistance.
Grievances grown to mountain height.
Valleys littered with lifeless promises.
Points of attack and counter-attack endless
as I watch darkened skies fill with burning
signals to comrades waiting at celestial lookouts.

MY DAUGHTER USED TO SING TO ME

It has been more than five years since Boko Haram captured hundreds of schoolgirls in Chibok, Nigeria. Many of them have not been found. Two years after the abduction, author Adaobi Tricia Nwaubani interviewed the blind mother of one of the kidnapped girls. She recalled how she missed her daughter singing to her. New York Times, April 17, 2016.

She began as if a thin reed
had kissed air or the way bamboo
shudder when they embrace in wind.

I always looked up when her first
tentative notes landed, as if
my skin were sheathed in velvet.

I could see her rocking, a jug of
water on her head, hands filled with
baskets—grain, goat milk, yellow squash.

I could predict our day from her
tone, timbre. Fortissimo or allegro.
Harmony or dissonance.

Now, sight silenced, I stand outside
at night, believing my daughter still
sings, her music refracted by the stars.

THE SKY IS CRYING

Reporters have been interviewing Somalis to try to determine the dates and numbers of civilians injured or killed in American military drone strikes. Recent US reports claim that only two civilians have died in drone attacks over the past two years, while outside observers such as Amnesty International report much higher numbers. Traumatized survivors and witnesses often cannot provide specific details that can be independently verified by neutral observers. Brian Costner, "Gaslighting An Entire Nation," New York Times, April 27, 2019.

*the sky is cryin'/look at the tears running down the street
—Gary Moore 1959, "The Sky Is Crying Blues"

I lived far from Mogadishu.
I am a goatherd. My village
curved along the Shabelle River,
its roads paved with dust and ashes.

At night, ancient stars and meteors
called out desert rhymes and rhythms.
We could not read or write but we
understood their backbeat language.

My name is Ali. I traveled
here to tell my story about
how our heavens have betrayed us.
Of how an azure firmament

dissolved to smoky flames before
me as my sister ground maize
and my ten year old nephew sang
to a scruffy black and white kid.

How the first explosion splintered
mud huts and meager garden plots
as the second hit its target—
a battered tan Toyota SUV

filled with regional emirs.
Months later, I still tremble at
high pitched notes, like a piccolo
or whine of mosquitoes. Even doves.

This city is too crowded, yet my
hamlet is a place of no return.
My family needs more than I have.
No one wants to bear my sorrows.

Others fared worse from Al Shabab,
from misplaced loyalties or missed
coordinates. Only some say
our losses will be acknowledged.

For me, each day's air is thick with
premonition. As I stroll down
city streets, I wonder if some
next intended mark walks near me.

I never look up, even when
I hear that piercing whistle—
the keening, impudent croon
of these bitter American Blues.

TALES OF MARIPOSA MIGRANTS

On Thursday, February 14, 2019, a federal judge threw out a lawsuit brought by the National Butterfly Center, a 100-acre wildlife preserve located in Mission, Texas on the Rio Grande border. The Center had challenged actions by the Department of Homeland Security to destroy land that is home to over 150 species of butterflies and other protected insects, birds and animals. In addition to driving heavy machinery into the Center's land, the lawsuit challenged harassment of Center visitors by DHS personnel. The proposed border wall would split the Center's land in half, cut off critical access to food and habitats and likely destroy many species that depend on this preserve for survival.

Bulldozers slice across
sandy *Rio Grande* shores.
They push past bush grasses
that hug river edges, even as
a flame vine vies with winged
visitors for pride of place.

We are tawny emperors,
monarchs, mexican blue
wings. We are an armada
of soldiers, four-spotted
sailors joined by mimosa
yellow sulphurs, ruby-spotted

swallowtails, gossamer
winged dragonflies as we
share tales on echinacea
blossoms in tones of rose
and gold. Other migrants
join us as we nuzzle up

to blue sage, buttonbush,
blackbrush, celadon olive
trees glazed like pottery
while luminescent bees
and flirty hummingbirds
embrace mauve mistflowers.

Once, we spoke of seasons,
not sanctuary. We did
not need lawyers to dispatch
heavy metal predators.
Now we see how easily
freedom mutates to slogan,

how divisions transform
beliefs into ghost languages
heard only in whispers.
As hypocrisy huddles
in chrysalis, innocence
no longer shelters us.

Our universe should have
no walls. Our flights should be
like a benediction.
Please tell the judges
how we rise, refreshed, from
our passionflower prayers.
How, at night, the flutter
of our wings conducts an
orchestra in the sky.

MODIGLIANI ON MARS

Elon Musk plans on taking
artists far out into deep space.

They must be experts at making
sense of elemental grace,

their pens and brushes quaking,
their airborne canvasses in place.

They must be star struck, their shaking
hands expected to embrace

visions unknown in waking
moments. They must be swift, in case

opportunities too breathtaking
to capture quickly, race

by before the artist's breaking
heart can dictate how to place

each drop of paint, each aching
line, each blot of color, trace

each burst of solar radiance, making
adjustments for stellar light, erase

all misplaced shadows. Such staking
out of skyborne masterpieces, braced

against weightlessness, is an undertaking
some cynical souls may find misplaced.

Many subjects for groundbreaking
artworks exist on earth—a carapace

for survival. Should artists really be escaping
gravity's pull? It feels like a disgrace

to fly them to the moon or mars, forsaking
mirrors they could hold up in this place

as our planet expires in heartbreaking
agony due to decisions we would not face.

IV. PRESENCE IN THE ABSENCE

"The reason why the universe is eternal is that it does not live for itself; it gives life to others as it transforms."

—Lao Tzu

LOOKING OUT AT 42nd STREET

City rhythms feel electric on my skin.
The Hudson River emits a slight smoky haze.
Hot summer air settles over geometric rooftops,
copper and glass vie for attention with neon lights.

The Hudson River emits a slight smoky haze
as I stare toward a distant horizon line.
Copper and glass vie for attention with neon lights
while helicopters flit above the water like summer insects.

As I stare toward a distant horizon line,
I wonder if every city denizen feels safe
while helicopters flit above the water like summer insects,
or if the urge to run and hide takes over.

I wonder if every city denizen feels safe
walking streetside in the sweltering afternoon
or if the urge to run and hide takes over
even as sunset ripples slowly across the sky.

Walking streetside in the sweltering afternoon,
people push past us staring down at bright images.
Even as sunset ripples across the sky,
camera phones are cradled like newborns.

People push past us, staring down at bright images.
Some would call this the center of the universe.
Camera phones are cradled like newborns
as memories are captured in distant clouds.

Some would call this the center of the universe,
but I believe we are just dancing on its surface.
As memories are captured in distant clouds,
city rhythms feel electric on my skin.

SPACECRAFT

Scholars have been debating the so-called "two-space rule," where two spaces follow a period, at least since modern word processors made variable width fonts widely available. Recently, psychologists at Skidmore College concluded that it is slightly easier to comprehend printed text when two spaces follow the end of a sentence. Washington Post *, May 4, 2018.*

scholars are studying space
 on the page

spaces between words
 spaces between sentences

if we punctuate our thoughts
 do we want two spaces

after every sentence
 or after every word

does our mind's eye relax
 more with added intervals

does the depth of our words
 increase when there is distance

what about spaces between people
 do our mistakes benefit from margins

how different is having some space
 from making enough room

if what you write down is a lie
 does it matter

how much space is left
 at the end of the line

KINDNESS

I've got a chipmunk problem in my yard.
The tiny furred creatures have popped up
everywhere, sending showers of dirt
into the air like it was Yellowstone.
I cannot kill them even though I want to.
They will not leave, though I have raged

at them, insulted them and their ancestors.
I am trying to be *kind*. Even in smallest ways.
As the known world self-destructs around me,
shards of optimism falling from the sky before
I even have a chance to look up to see what has
shifted us off our comfortable axis.

My neighbor brings a *havahart* trap
so I can remove the invaders *kindly*.
He baits it with peanut butter.
Soon the trap has a frightened
occupant. I cannot bear to look for fear
of crying. The prisoner is soon relocated.

The trap is replaced. A new chipmunk takes
the bait. He too is repatriated to new territory.
Capture and repeat. Each day, unending
arrays of innocents are tempted by
creamy nut paste. Soon enough, I begin
to worry about babes left behind in tunnels,

about mothers and fathers, grieving for lost children.
One day a chipmunk plants itself on my deck
and looks in through the window. My *kind* self
huddles behind the blind. I will not make eye contact.
This is the *humane* way, I say to myself, even as I begin
to imagine each trapped rodent wearing an orange

jumpsuit as interrogators gather nearby with pen
and paper waiting for the inevitable confessions.

One night, the trap is sprung, its detainee freed from
house arrest. I am thrilled. Then I learn a bear
has likely done it. Probably thanked me for
an easy meal. Still no *kindness* in my yard.

This is how it always begins.
Good intentions vanishing
like some dying star, rationalizations
reverberating across celestial centuries.
Turns out it is our unwavering belief
in our own self-righteousness that is the trap.

DIAMONDS IN THE SOULS OF OUR VIEWS

In 2008, an asteroid, Almahata Sitta, exploded in the sky above Sudan's Nubian desert. More than 600 rock fragments were discovered by student searchers from the University of Kartoum. Scientists recently confirmed that these meteorites contain tiny diamonds which, in turn, contain even smaller impurities, known as inclusions, formed over 4.5 billion years ago when their host planet—possibly as large as Mars—was destroyed in a massive explosion. These extraterrestrial space diamonds were likely formed under the same extreme pressures and high temperatures that exist in the interior of any planet but astronomers have been unable to trace them to any parent bodies in the Earth's known solar system. New York Times, *April 30, 2018, A12.*

Gems rain down from wide desert skies.
Searchers race to collect evidence
of asteroidal factures, as if
Tiffany's had been suddenly
unlocked, its crown jewels
left untended, arrayed on velvet.

Space scientists inspect these rocks
like DNA detectives. Each
sparkle shocks as, piece by piece,
a story emerges into light,
the way a suspect's reluctant
confession reshapes a crime scene.

As deeply hidden tales go,
these baubles may hold more secrets
than we care to know. Lost planets.
Ancient eras. Cinematic
crashes. Spectacular debris.
Tears of gods shine like diamonds.

THE SOUNDS OF TRUTH VANISHING
(A Lesson for Our Time)

In the end, truth vanished too quietly.
There was a certain wonder to it all.
We stared out at distant specks of light
as though we had drifted into space.

There was a certain wonder to it all
as we imagined it still flickering,
as though we had drifted into space,
while once familiar places faded away.

As we imagined it still flickering
like echoes of a gentle chorale,
while once familiar places faded away,
we struggled to recall the journey.

Like echoes of a gentle chorale,
we began to keep tiny secrets.
We struggled to recall the journey,
starting with small adornments to our own histories.

We began to keep tiny secrets
long before PT Barnum stepped onstage,
starting with small adornments to our own histories
as if crocheting rubies onto a hangman's rope.

Long before PT Barnum stepped onstage,
we tried to add hints of hopeful sparkle,
as if crocheting rubies onto a hangman's rope,
mournful ends traded for cheery platitudes.

We tried to add hints of hopeful sparkle,
discarding facts like childish thoughts,
mournful ends traded for cheery platitudes.
Soon we could only hear what pleased us.

Discarding facts like childish thoughts,

we chose nicer words to match new visions.
Soon we could hear only what pleased us
as the known world slipped away.

We chose nicer words to match new visions.
Amazed at how far we had traveled
as the known world slipped away,
we sometimes said *Remember when* ….

Amazed at how far we had traveled,
we met those who did not understand why
we sometimes said *Remember when*….
In the end, truth vanished too quietly.

RINGS OF FIRE

The Laboratory of Tree Ring Research at the University of Arizona,
Tucson, founded by astronomer A.E. Douglass in the 1930's, studies
connections between sunspots and climate reflected in tree rings and
cores. The Lab contains more than half a million samples. As trees age,
their rings circling the trunks expand each year. Each ring stores data
about the year's temperatures, precipitation, jet stream behavior,
fire activity and other extreme climate events. Tree rings contain
elements carbon which reflects the interaction of cosmic and nitrogen
at various points throughout the tree's history.

Tree rings turn out to be nature's
Dear Diary. They can tell us when rain
refused to end and when it stopped its fall.
Like Johnny Cash, forests know how
fast a heart can break, how heat
of fire can *burn, burn, burn.*

A Bosnian pine tree named Adonis
has stood in Greece for a millennium.
It speaks to jet streams, hears star secrets.
In Colorado, a twenty year drought sets
records as river waters evaporate.
Blue spruce chronicle their migration.

When volcanoes blew their tops or desert
climates pushed north like arid armadas,
bristlecone pines recorded each maneuver.
As nomads scattered like their failed crops
of corn, beans and squash, their exodus
story was written in concentric coils.

A chiaroscuro of cosmic rays
and solar flares dance across Japanese
cedar tree circles. They carry messages
as prescient as ancient Anglo-Saxon
Chronicles or Dead Sea Scrolls. Collapsed
empires etched in grains of wood like poetry.

POLARIZATION

who says our world
is fractured
that we have nothing
in common

coast to coast
bound together by
amber grains
waving
plains of fruit
corn as high as
melting mountains
lakes turned to
desert flowers
then sandstone memories

soon enough we will tire
of watching polar bears
stranded on melted floes
growing thin as icicles

but by then
assuming we are still
able to talk
about anything at all

everyone will be
sinking instead
of swimming
can you imagine us
altogether now
as we try to breathe
underwater
will we mouth words
of wonder of anger
or apology

INTERNET CARAVAN

NASA announced recently that it is now possible to conduct a Google Maps search of Martian terrain using extensive photographs of the planet taken by cameras installed on rover satellites that have been sent into space over more than 30 years. Six Mars rovers have successfully landed there, including the Curiosity which remains operational after its 2012 landing.

Google Maps can transport us out to Mars.
Soon, we'll play hide and seek on old dark stars,
explore hills and valleys on distant moons,
learn if Saturn's deserts have ice-filled dunes.

As we traverse across the Milky Way,
we might zoom in on exciting places
that could seduce us if we need to pray
for kinder landscapes, veiled by hope's traces.

We've long suspected worlds more generous
than ours are spinning someplace, offering
strands of optimism more plenteous
than meteor showers. No suffering.

Scanning space, we see we could be lifted
past despair if our perspectives shifted.

ESCAPE VELOCITY

In physics, escape velocity is the minimum speed needed for a free object to escape from the gravitational influence of a massive body. It is slower the further away from the body an object is, and slower for less massive bodies. The escape velocity from Earth is about 11.186 km/s at the surface. Wikipedia

I.
shouldn't we be
plotting our grand
getaways   night
often works best
though daybreak can
sometimes provide
cover   one blends
in with rush of
crowds on their way
to purposeful
tasks energy's din
a canopy

my mother sat
for many days
at a small town
bus depot   she
meant to pass her
cash to the clerk
dreamt of how far
it might take her
lacking baggage
or IOUs
tried to picture
her light new life

once tempted how
hard it is to
stay tethered to
our small patches

of space we stare
hard at windows
measure doorways
calculate weight
height depth distance
keep mind journals
which cannot be
used against us

as we crawl through
mangrove forests
and cypress swamps
guided only
by distant stars
and drinking gourds
songs of freedom
propel us toward
some distant point
where we picture
our brand new selves
soaring unfettered

II.
our sad planet
sinks dries burns up
cyclone winds roar
dry land recedes
pollinators
vanish by the
thousands
species follow
soon after   an
eye blink is all
it takes as fields
fill with prayers

some days I am

tempted to ask
god about an
afterlife   maybe
she can spare some
angel who is
out of work feels
lazy or kind
who is good at
explanations
maybe I will
feel prepared

with a backbeat
of winged voices
to aid us as
we abscond to
elevations
higher than we
know now   safer
perhaps or just
different we
might join Elon
Musk in space flight
laughing all the

way to Mars while
our blue planet
turns pale as ash
maybe as we
steal away to
newer planes of
lightness we would
have a minute
to ask god if
she knew on day
seven what troubles
we would conjure

III.

I have always
loved Houdini
how he managed
disappearance
as if he just
slipped on some
dinner jacket
or elegant
Harry Blackstone
who could send a
caged canary
to another sphere

or levitate
a princess from
her fainting couch
once my father
took me to watch
Mr Blackstone
float a lightbulb
in a darkened
theatre as we
followed its arc
as if possessed
dreaming of the ride

the *idea* was
the magic
breaking away
from gravity's
pull leaning in
to places no
one had measured
or predicted
to spaces where
dimensions might

not be confined
to only three

when I grew up
women did not
fly or lead space
missions they were
practical, down
to earth, nurtured
by nature they
stayed put even
when ground gave way
no wonder then that
so many of us
want to take flight

PRESENCE IN THE ABSENCE

On April 10, 2019, Scientists from around the world released the first image of a "supermassive" black hole at the center of a galaxy over 55 million light years from earth. The galaxy, Messier 87, is located in the constellation Virgo. The image was isolated using a network of synchronized telescopes across the globe that captured high frequency radio waves. Data captured by these laboratories represented the equivalent of 2 billion high quality photographs. Washington Post, April 11, 2019, A1, 20.

Black holes have our attention
again. We still know little
or nothing. They are consummate
known unknowns, as Rumsfeld said.

An image haunts us as we guess
at portraits of bending space, our
breath catches mid-inhale, as we
ruminate on combustion.

Or collapse. I had a lover
once who made me feel I could do
both at the same time—plummet from
heat to nothingness in seconds.

How I gravitated from flame
to black ice still amazes
all these light years later. Now,
my days gravitate toward sun

but I can still be devoured by
past lives—places where memory
curves inward, where one tries to
read a future from stardust grains.

That is why we seek out things
we cannot know or remember.

Ignorance, like rings of fire, may
devour us, but shadows of faith adhere.

NEW HORIZONS

*On January 1, 2019, NASA's New Horizons spacecraft, launched in
January, 2006, entered the outer reaches of Earth's solar system, the
Kuiper Belt, passing Ultima Thule, a rocky object believed to date from
the formation of the solar system more than 4.6 billion years ago. The
Kuiper Belt, filled with icy bodies, is so far away that it takes more than
six hours for signals to reach Earth traveling at the speed of light.
Objects in the outer solar system are colored an extreme red.*

Ice is red here. Blood red.
Lava red. Forest fire red.
Cold sears like flame. Or so
one might think from afar.

They say it all began
here in this distant chunk
of frozen rocks. Our sun
lies four billion miles out.

We could be wrong about
everything. Gravity's pull
is different in new orbits.
Patience may be required.

Warped by turmoil, we've turned
outward, searching sky signs
for cosmic engagements,
for hints of original sins.

ACKNOWLEDGEMENTS:

The poems "STAR WARS (FROM A TO Z)" and "GOLDILOCKS AND…" were first published in Volume 17 of *The Offbeat Magazine* in May 2017. An earlier version of the poem "EVENING STAR was published by *The Raven's Perch* in January, 2017. The poem "PERSEID METEOR SHOWERS" was first published in Volume 2 of *Into the Void Magazine* in September, 2016. The poem "THE MATHEMATICS OF PARKING" was published on June 16, 2017 on the blog http//:womenatwoodstock.com. It also appears in *An Apple In Her Hand*, an anthology of writings by the Hudson Valley Women's Writing Group, published by Codhill Press in January, 2019. The poem "THE SOUNDS OF TRUTH VANISHING," was short-listed for the 2018 Fish Publishing Prize and also appears in *An Apple In Her Hand*. The poem also appears as part of a poem series, "REVERBERATIONS," published by *Junto Magazine* in December, 2018. "KILANOVAS" appears in the author's poetry chapbook, *A Woman of a Certain Age* published in September, 2018 by Finishing Line Press. The poem "KINDNESS," first published by *The New Verse News* on June 21, 2018, also appears in "A Woman of a Certain Age" and in *An Apple In Her Hand*. The poem was nominated for a 2019 Pushcart Prize. The poems "THE UMBRA AROUND US," "FISSION" and "ICE SKATING ON THE MOON" were published by *Voice of Eve* in November, 2018. The poem "SLIPPING BELOW THE SURFACE" was published by *In Layman's Terms* in November, 2018. The poem 'LOOKING OUT AT 42ND STREET," was published in *Songs of Eretz Poetry Review* in March, 2018. The poem "NEW HORIZONS" was published on January 8, 2019 by *The New Verse News*. The poem "PIANO MAN" first appeared in the fall 2019 issue of *Split Rock Review*. The poem "TRAVELS TO THE VALLEY OF LOST THINGS" won First Prize in the 2019 poetry contest sponsored by *Slippery Elm Literary Magazine* and appears in the 2019 issue of the magazine. The poem "PRESENCE IN THE ABSENCE" was published on April 12, 2019 by *The New Verse News*. The poem "PORTRAIT OF A GHAZAN STARGAZER," won Honorable Mention in the 87th Annual *Writer's Digest* Writing Competition (Non-Rhyming Poetry), and appears in *An Apple In Her Hand*.

PERSONAL APPRECIATIONS:

The beautiful cover art, "Biocriticals No. 1," is the work of my friend and former neighbor, Betsy Stewart, an award-winning, nationally and internationally recognized artist. Betsy's work appears in museums, galleries, corporate collections, embassies, hotels and other world-wide venues. Betsy's beautiful piece examines microscopic and macroscopic subjects often hidden from the naked eye, visualizing the origins of life that might exist in a drop of water or as a system in our vast cosmos. As her web site explains, she is "fascinated with the workings of the universe." Her "Biocritical" series, in particular, "considers the ambiguity and interconnectivity between those worlds" and was a perfect choice to represent the ideas I wanted to express in this volume of poetry. To see more of Betsy's work go to her website at www.betsystewart.com.

I am deeply grateful to my sister, the artist Elizabeth Anastasia O'Melveny, for her creative work to create the final cover design for this poetry book as well as for her creation of and continual improvements to my poetry website. As always, my dear friends and trusted readers, have given me great encouragement and feedback along the way. Thanks especially to my spouse, Susan Waysdorf, and to Mary Gawronski, Karen Mandell and members of the Hudson Valley Women's Writing Group who always bring my writing to a higher level—Colleen Geraghty, Kit Goldpaugh, Eileen Howard, Tana Miller, Jan Zlotnik-Schmidt and Kappa Waugh. Finally, but by no means last in importance, my heartfelt thanks to the brilliant poet, author and professor Charlotte Pence, whose editorial guidance and creative support were invaluable to me as I made the journey leading to publication of this volume of poems. Charlotte's understanding of the interplay between science and poetry made her the perfect editorial guide for this collection and her own beautiful poems on topics of family, the cosmos and the environment are always inspirational. For more information about Charlotte's work, go to www.charlottepence.com.

Mary K O'Melveny, lives with her wife, Susan Waysdorf, in Washington DC and Woodstock, NY. After retiring from a distinguished career as a labor rights lawyer in New York City and Washington, DC, where she represented workers, labor unions and political prisoners, Mary returned to writing poetry—an interest she had not seriously pursued since college. Mary received many peer-based honors and awards during her legal career and authored articles for law review journals and many legal conference papers and training materials. Mary's poetry has been published in both print and on-line journals and anthologies, including *Aji Magazine, In Layman' Terms, Into the Void, The Write Place at the Write Time, FLARE: The Flagler Review, The Offbeat, The New Reader, Split Rock Review, Allegro Poetry Magazine, West Texas Review, The Voices Project* and *Slippery Elm Literary Journal.*

Mary is a member of various writing organizations and groups, including The Hudson Valley Women's Writing Group whose recently published anthology, *An Apple In Her Hand*, is available from Codhill Press. In 2017, Mary's poem "Cease Fire" won the Raynes Poetry Competition sponsored by *Jewish Currents Magazine*. She also was a Finalist for the 2017 Pangaea Prize sponsored by *The Poet's Billow*. In 2018, Mary was a finalist in the Tom Howard/Margaret Reid Poetry Competition sponsored by Winning Writers and was short-listed for the Fish Publishing Prize judged by Ellen Bass. In 2019, Mary's poem "Travels to the Valley of Lost Things" was awarded the Slippery Elm Poetry Prize. Mary's poetry chapbook, *A Woman of a Certain Age*, was published in September, 2018 by Finishing Line Press.

CPSIA information can be obtained
at www.ICGtesting.com
Printed in the USA
BVHW030242250120
570399BV00004B/22